Trusting That God Will Provide

BY JANET KOBOBEL GRANT

WOMEN OF FAITH℠
BIBLE STUDY SERIES

Women of the Bible

Trusting That God Will Provide

A Study on Ruth

Janet Kobobel Grant

Foreword by Barbara Johnson

Judith Couchman, *General Editor*

GRAND RAPIDS, MICHIGAN 49530 USA

We want to hear from you. Please send your comments about this book to us in care of the address below. Thank you.

GRAND RAPIDS, MICHIGAN 49530 USA

WWW.ZONDERVAN.COM

Trusting That God Will Provide
Formerly titled *Ruth*
Copyright © 1999 by Women of Faith, Inc.

Judith Couchman, General Editor

Requests for information should be addressed to:

Zondervan, *Grand Rapids, Michigan 49530*

ISBN 0-310-24786-1

Interior design by Sherri Hoffman

Printed in the United States of America

*To my mom, who exemplified God's generous
provision through her sacrifices for me*

Contents

Acknowledgments

*B*ouquets of thank-yous are presented to:

Robin Jones Gunn, who taught me more about fiction than she will ever know and who dug through boxes of books to find resources for me.

Alan Scholes, who dropped everything but the phone when I called to ask technical questions.

The Plot & Blot Writing Society that brainstormed ideas and rained on some of my writing to enrich the soil.

My husband, Loch, who talked about Ruth more than he probably ever wanted to.

Foreword

*W*hen I think of the story of Ruth, I think of the song "Bringing in the Sheaves." When I was a child, I usually sang, "Bringing in the *cheese*," because I sure didn't know what *sheaves* were. I do remember one verse, though, that went like this: "Sowing in the sunshine, sowing in the shadows, fearing neither clouds or winter's chilling breeze . . . by and by the harvest, and the labor ended, we shall come rejoicing, bringing in the sheaves."

Rejoicing? Ruth must have had her share of doubts about leaving her homeland not knowing how she might survive in another country. Faith doesn't completely replace fear. Loyalty won't eradicate insecurity. Ruth was alone and probably afraid as she gathered leftover stalks of barley along an open field. But Ruth had made a decision to believe in God and live among his people in spite of how things looked. She focused her eyes on the invisible. Then she put her arms and hands to work! Most likely, she toted the bundles of grain on her back, or in a fabric sling around her shoulders as she bent over hour after hour in the hot sun. Rejoicing? Bringing in the sheaves was back-breaking work!

What Ruth didn't know was that Boaz, owner of the barley field, had ordered his harvesters to pull stalks of barley from their own bundles and drop them on the ground for her to find. God arranged this, honoring Ruth's willingness to accept every opportunity to prosper, no matter how insignificant. She was to have not only enough to survive, she was to have an abundance.

The Lord created you and I with the ability to overcome by *attitude*, rather than *latitude* (where we stand on the social scale). Ruth decided to go for life, to glean its simple pleasures, to harvest joy even in a strange land. God provided not only her physical needs; he provided for her spiritual and emotional needs, too. He gave her the companionship of a godly mother-in-law, and later, the love of a good man, children of her own — and a rich legacy. Ruth became the great-grandmother of King David. She couldn't have come further from her poverty-stricken days bundling sheaves in a dusty field.

In her days of rejoicing, I think Ruth probably discovered that Boaz had been dropping extra barley just for her. Someday, you'll discover God is doing the same for you. In the middle of your struggle to survive — emotionally, financially, through sickness or bad relationships — whatever it is, he is providing *more* than you need. Yes, your back may be aching, your heart may be breaking, but put your hands to work! Pick up hope and joy and bind them into sheaves! Elevate your attitude with gratitude! Look around, there is laughter over there! And love all around you — so much you can hardly keep up with it.

As you study the book of Ruth through this beautifully conceived Bible study, pay attention. Don't lose a single grain of truth. God wants to show you something. Be willing to receive like Ruth. Oh, and don't forget to have fun while you're bringing in the "cheese." You're on your way to abundant life. Start rejoicing!

— Barbara Johnson

About This Study

*E*veryone loves a captivating story. It can prompt laughter, tears, nods of the head, even thoughtful silence. Best of all, a good story teaches us how to live better. It doles out guidelines, points to pitfalls, and inspires us toward heart-changing action. It infuses the ordinary with meaning and the tragic with truth.

In this Women of Faith discussion guide you'll explore one of those poignant stories. Through the life of Ruth, a biblical woman with an intriguing dilemma, you'll learn how God can work in the world, in the lives of his people, and in your particular circumstances. Each of the six sessions unfolds her story, compares it to yours, and initiates a group discussion that hopefully invokes spiritual growth and life-related applications.

To most effectively use this discussion guide with your group, consider organizing your time as follows.

BEFORE THE GROUP SESSION

Before attending a meeting, take time alone to evaluate your life and prepare for the next group discussion. During this time read and ponder the following sections of the discussion guide.

- *Opening Narrative.* Each week you'll be ushered into another chapter of Ruth's story. This fiction narrative introduces her unusual circumstances and helps you envision how Ruth felt, and perhaps what she did, as the events around her unfolded. It can get you thinking about the story before the group assembles, and whet your appetite for what happens next.
- *Setting the Stage.* Based on Ruth's story and the session's theme, think about your life. The questions and suggested activities can help you consider the following: How am I doing in this area? How do I feel about it? What do I want to do or change? How does this affect my spiritual life? Be honest with yourself and God, asking him to teach you through Ruth's story.

The heart of this guide focuses on gathering for discussion and encouragement. It allows time to study the Bible, apply its truths to your lives, and spend time praying. Of course, you can add whatever else fits the nature of your group, such as a time for a "coffee klatch" or catching up on each other's lives. Whatever you decide, reserve about an hour for the next three sessions.

- *Discussing Ruth's Story.* In this section read and discuss a biblical passage that captures the remarkable events of Ruth's life. Though it centers on the facts of God's Word, at times you'll read between the lines and suggest people's feelings, motivations, and character qualities to gain insights to their actions. Still, you can answer these questions without compromising the biblical text.

  To best manage this discussion time, you can follow these steps:

  1. Ask one woman to read out loud the opening narrative, if it seems appropriate. If not, skip this step.
  2. As a group read aloud the Bible text stated at the beginning of the section. Take turns reading verses so each woman participates.
  3. Discuss the questions together, consulting specific verses from the text as needed.

- *Behind the Scenes.* This section provides background information related to the biblical text. It enlightens the story's culture and history, and helps you answer the discussion questions. You can refer to this section as you discuss Ruth's story.

- *Sharing Your Story.* How does Ruth's story apply to your life? As a group you can answer the questions in this section, relating the events of her life to your own and uncovering nuggets of practical application. These questions target group sharing rather than personal contemplation.

- *Prayer Matters.* To conclude your session use these ideas to guide the group in prayer, especially focusing on individual needs.

AFTER A MEETING

Since spiritual growth doesn't end with your small group gathering, try these suggestions to extend learning into the next week and encourage one-on-one relationships. However, these sections are optional, depending on your interest and schedule.

- *After Hours.* These activities help apply the lesson's principles to everyday life. You can complete them with a friend or by yourself.
- *Words to Remember.* After you return home, consider memorizing the selected Bible verses for encouragement and guidance.

In addition, the back of the book presents a Leader's Guide to help your group's facilitator pilot the discussion. To ensure that everyone contributes to the conversation, it's best to keep the group at six to eight participants. If the membership increases, consider splitting into smaller groups during the discussion times and gathering together for the concluding prayer.

However you organize the meeting, keep the emphasis on discussion — sharing ideas, needs, and questions, rather than striving for a consensus of opinion. That's the pleasure of a good story. It stimulates thinking and reflects our inner selves so along with Ruth we can become women of faith.

— Judith Couchman, General Editor

Introduction

The Book of Ruth reminds me of a play with three central characters (Ruth, Naomi, Boaz), four acts (or chapters), simple props (some barley, a blanket, a sandal), and lots of drama. Ruth, the main character, is distinguished by being one of only two women with a book of the Bible named after her. And by her generosity of heart.

Ruth shows us how big her heart is when, at the beginning of the play, she travels away from all she knows. She leaves her country, her language, her friends and family, her customs, her gods, and the grave sites of her husband, brother-in-law, and father-in-law. Then she opens her heart to her mother-in-law, a new country, a new language, new customs, and a new God. Ruth doesn't hold back any part of her heart but pledges to Naomi, "Where you go I will go, and where you stay I will stay. Your people will be my people and your God my God. Where you die I will die, and there I will be buried. May the LORD deal with me, be it ever so severely, if anything but death separates you and me" (Ruth 1:16–17).

Such a promise is not for the fainthearted! Ruth doesn't whine, "Well, I don't know what it will be like to live in Bethlehem. I'm used to big cities. Don't know if a small town suits me. And Naomi, you've been real down in the mouth ever since all your relatives died. Now, I've been patient with you so far, but if you don't snap out of it pretty soon, I might not stay around. And, speaking of staying around, you haven't exactly offered any concrete ideas on how we're going to find a place to stay or food to eat. You've got to pull your weight in this relationship, you know. Keeping all this in mind, Naomi, I'm going to take a chance and go with you. But don't forget; this is temporary."

Not Ruth. She pledges undying loyalty. She has a big heart. And a big faith for one so young in the business of believing.

In act two Ruth applies heart — and hands — to shape the future. As widows in the Hebrew culture, she and Naomi are in a precarious place — vulnerable, poor, and without a male relative's protection. So Ruth humbles her heart, bends her back, and develops calluses on her hands as she follows the barley harvesters, picking up what they have dropped. If her heart longed for happier days in her old hometown, she doesn't let on.

Instead, in the upcoming scenes her heart wins the favor of the landowner and eventually his heart as well. Soon Ruth finds her hands busily caring for their newborn and her heart entwined with the love that surrounds her — from her husband, her mother-in-law, and her God. Ruth has discovered that, even in a new land, with no one to protect her and no resources to draw upon, God will provide. He will provide through other people, through her own initiative, and from the laws woven into the fabric of society.

So Ruth's story has a happy ending. She follows her heart, trusting God despite what she has seen. And God comes through in surprising ways.

Through Ruth's story we learn that if the heart aches, God can satisfy its longing. If we have an empty pantry, he can fill it. If we have bitter relatives, God can show himself good even to them. If we feel vulnerable and unprotected, God will shelter us under his wings. If we have a sorrowful past, God can turn it into a joyful future. All this, if we will give him our wholehearted devotion.

Like Ruth, you may need God's provision and don't know which way to turn or how to trust him. Be encouraged. You can develop a courageous and faith-filled heart, even in the face of heart-stopping realities, by learning how Ruth played her part in God's drama. So let's move into the auditorium. The lights are dimming, and the play is about to begin . . .

— Janet Kobobel Grant

R U T H — *Trusting That God Will Provide for You*

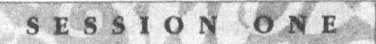

Tough Choices

*When times are difficult,
we can trust the Lord.*

The sky metamorphosed slowly from gray to pink. The three women, wearing heavy veils that announced their widowhood, trudged along without speaking.

Ruth sighed. She and her sister-in-law, Orpah, had started out the journey from Moab to Bethlehem trying to act cheerful and enthusiastic. They had sung songs until they couldn't think of any more. Then they sang all the old ones again until they were sick of them. Then they told all the jokes they could remember. Eventually they fell silent and just walked. Ruth felt as though they had plodded forward for a very long time. But they still had a long way to go, and this was only the second day of their trek.

Ruth's calf muscles ached. The pack on her back rubbed sores created the day before, and the weariness sitting on her shoulders lingered from a sleepless night. She had known many such wakeful nights since her husband had died.

Even now her mind turned to thoughts of Mahlon, with his large brown eyes, slow smile, and slender fingers. He'd had a tender spirit that she depended on. But his gentleness hadn't saved him from the fever that quickly wasted his body and stole his life — the same fever that took his brother's life. She pushed the images of Mahlon's hot face and fiery eyes out of her mind. She didn't want to remember that part. She would remember him before the illness. Before widowhood.

"Widow," Ruth softly uttered the word, still trying to assimilate it as her new designation. It was a willowy word without substance that swayed with each breeze of adversity. Much like she felt without Mahlon.

She glanced over to Orpah. Pretty Orpah, of the dancing eyes and feet, was lost in her own thoughts. She didn't seem as pretty now — now that the music had left her life.

They felt sad and lost, both of them. But no more so than Ruth's widowed mother-in-law, Naomi, who trudged on slightly ahead of the young women. Maybe she was eager to be home in Bethlehem, out of Moab. Or maybe she was pushed forward by a sorrow that propelled her like a prod in the back. Naomi had always stood rod straight, back unbent, but now she walked with stooped shoulders, worn down by the burden of so many losses. Her spirit seemed almost broken.

The two young women were moving to a new town because of Naomi. That she might find consolation with her old neighbors. That she might sit around the evening fire with friends who remembered more joyful times — before the famine caused Naomi's family to move, before her husband had died, before she had lost her sons, before ten hard years had passed. Maybe the light in Naomi's eyes, her lively spirit, and her lovely smile would return. And maybe she would find her God again, the God whom she seemed to have lost. The God she had believed in wholeheartedly when Ruth first met her.

For Naomi, Ruth had packed her few belongings and set her mind to move to Bethlehem, to give up her gods, to become the foreigner — and to be seen as a heathen one at that.

For Naomi you will do this, Ruth told herself, shooing away a fly. The sun began gathering its heat and directing it onto the widows who had so far to walk. *So she can find life and her God again, you will do this ...*

 *Setting the Stage*

WHICH WAY IS HOME?

Like Ruth, Naomi, and Orpah, the characters in *The Wizard of Oz* embark on a quest that requires courage, caring, smarts, and a longing for home. This week before the group meeting, think about the Oz story, or if you have time, rent a videotape of the movie or read the book.

Based on the tape, book, or your memory of the story, think about the adversities that each of the main characters faces. Write down the ways the cowardly lion overcomes his fears, the tin man discovers his heart, the scarecrow finds his brain, and Dorothy finds her way home.

RUTH — *Trusting That God Will Provide for You*

Then answer the following questions:

- Which character do you identify with the most?

- What adversities do you face?

- What keeps you from believing in yourself?

- What tornadoes have separated you from "home"?

- What do you need to feel "at home" with yourself spiritually, mentally, and emotionally?

- What might be the "yellow brick road" in your life?

- What clues does the movie offer to help you to overcome your fears, discover your heart, develop the confidence to use your brain, and find your way home?

Write down what needs to change in your life for you to be "at home" with yourself. Prayerfully set goals of how you can reach home. Commit your discoveries to God. Ask him to work in your life through Ruth's story.

MANY CHOICES

Ruth steps out of her culture and into the murky waters of an unknown future. The only visible stepping-stones have uninviting names: widow, poverty, foreigner. She has a difficult journey ahead of her, with many choices to make. But the biggest and foremost choice centers on whether to believe in God and his ability to provide for her.

Before you begin the discussion, read the Bible text, Ruth 1:1–18.

1. Ruth 1:1 establishes the time in which Ruth lived. What insights does Judges 2:10–19 offer you about this era? How might it feel to be a widow in this culture?

2. After reading Ruth 1:2–5 and the Behind the Scenes section, "Unholy Neighbors," on page 24, do you think Elimelech was trusting God to provide when he moved his family to Moab to escape the famine? Why or why not?

3. Ask three women to role-play the parts of Ruth, Naomi, and Orpah. Have the three of them hold a press conference, with the others in the group playing the part of the Moabite press. Ask the women questions about their leaving Moab and moving to Bethlehem emphasizing questions about how the women feel concerning this relocation. As they answer, have the press write down the emotions each woman expresses. When the press conference is over, add any other emotions the group can think of that Ruth, Naomi, and Orpah may have been feeling.

4. What choices did each of the women face after their husbands died? What was difficult about each choice?

5. What does Orpah and Ruth's response to Naomi in verses 8–10 tell you about these daughters-in-law? How could the emotions you listed in question three affect their response?

6. What does Naomi reveal about her relationship to God in verses 11–13? What does Ruth's response in verses 14–18 reveal about her view of God? How might these opinions about God affect the two younger women's choices?

Behind the Scenes

UNHOLY NEIGHBORS

Moab's relationship to Israel is difficult to define. In some ways Moab was closely affiliated with Israel, with the Moabite language and writing traditions similar to Hebrew. But in Israel's mind Moab had an unholy beginning. The man Moab was born through the incestuous union of Lot and his eldest daughter (Genesis 19:30–37).

Also, while the Israelites were traveling to the Promised Land from Egypt, the king of Moab, Balak, was frightened by them. Consequently, he hired the prophet Balaam to pronounce a curse on Israel (Numbers 22–24). Because of this act, God commanded that no Moabite would be allowed to enter the Lord's congregation (Deuteronomy 23:3–4). However, marriage with a Moabite woman wasn't forbidden in the law (Deuteronomy 7:1–4), so Ruth's and Orpah's marriages to Jewish men weren't shunned by the people of Bethlehem.

EENIE, MEENIE . . .

When difficulties darken our doorstep, hard choices confront us. How can we — like Ruth, Orpah, and Naomi — decide what to do? How can we learn to lean on God and trust him to provide what we desperately need?

One place to start is understanding the word *provision,* which derives from a Latin word meaning "foreseeing, forethought, precaution, providing." God gives forethought to our needs, foresees the choices we make, and takes precaution to insure we'll be provided for. What blessed assurance that he is trustworthy!

1. What is the most difficult choice you've made in regard to God's provision for you?

2. Look at the list of emotions from question three in Discussing Ruth's Story. Circle the emotions you tend to feel when hardships invade your life. Add to the list any others you feel.

3. How can these emotions cloud our judgment about God's provision? How can they clarify what we should do?

4. What choices about God and his provision can we make as we pass through a hard time?

5. List at least five of God's characteristics to remember as we cast about to make a difficult choice and trust his provision. Look up the following verses to stimulate your thinking: Joshua 21:45; Psalm 117; Proverbs 18:10; Matthew 19:26; Hebrews 13:5–6.

6. The apostle Paul writes in Philippians 4:19: "And my God will meet all your needs according to his glorious riches in Christ Jesus." How can we truly believe and trust that God is faithful in his promise to provide our needs? What actions would express our trust?

Believing steadfastly in God while we face hard situations and choices is one of the greatest challenges to our spiritual lives. But setting our minds on God's character helps to steer us in the right direction.

Prayer Matters

UNITED HEARTS

As a group write a prayer about choices to trust God's provision. Include some of the insights you've gained today. For example, the emotions we feel, the questions we have about God, and the longings we experience.

Now divide into pairs. If you feel comfortable, share with each other a needed provision or difficult choice in your life. Pray for each other by reading the just-written group prayer. If you've shared hardships and choices, insert specific requests for those issues as you read the prayer.

After Hours

YESTERDAY, TODAY, TOMORROW

With a friend or as a group: Seven hundred years ago a French queen named Jeanne d'Evreux commissioned a prayer book for herself, which is now safely kept at the New York Metropolitan Museum of Art. The book is three-and-a-half inches high and two-and-a-half inches wide. Several miniaturists painted depictions from Christ's life that appear among the prayers. A liturgical calendar opens the book and contains paintings appropriate for the various months — cutting wheat in July, stomping grapes in September. Whimsical sketches appear in the margins of some pages. While the queen's prayer book sounds marvelous, the idea behind the book is even more so.

Get together with a friend or a group and create opening pages for personal prayer scrapbooks or journals. Buy a notebook or scrapbook. Bring a bag of craft items to share. Include glue, stamps, scissors, colored paper, colored pens or pencils . . . let your imagination roam. Brainstorm ideas together. Make it a creative, crafty time. And remember, the point isn't to make a masterpiece but to create a book that enhances the joy of your times with God. Few of us are artists — or even artistic — but all of us have unique and wonderful relationships with God.

Later, as you record in the book your prayers, requests, praises, special Scriptures, or memorable phrases that speak to your heart, it will reflect your spiritual journey as you learn to trust God and his provision. Along the way keep using stickers, stamps, even your own margin illustrations, to personalize and express how you feel.

On your own: Create three columns vertically on a piece of paper. Label them "Yesterday," "Today," and "Tomorrow." In each column write down a hardship you have faced (Yesterday), you are facing (Today), and you will face (Tomorrow), particularly in the area of provision.

Then complete these sentences for each column:

- I wish . . .

- If only . . .

- What if . . .

- But then . . .

- I believe . . .

- Thank God . . .

As you look over the sheet, prayerfully place the regrets you've expressed in God's lap. Then discuss your concerns with him. End with praises for what he has done, despite the pain you have experienced or anticipate. Choose to believe the best of God and that he has the best waiting for you.

Words to Remember

ASKING FOR GRACE

Let us then approach the throne of grace with confidence, so that
we may receive mercy and find grace to help us in our time of need.

— Hebrews 4:16

Challenges Galore

We can persevere as we
wait for God's provision.

*A*s Ruth pulled the pot off the fire in her new home, she took a deep breath to keep from speaking up. *This isn't how I pictured it at all,* she thought, moving around the circle of wizened widows and pouring more of the hot drink into their cups.

"I'm telling you, Naomi, the famine was hard — and long. Lost Amos and Eli the fourth year." The woman who spoke made a clicking sound with her tongue as if scolding God for allowing such losses.

"But that year was nothing compared to the seventh and eighth," added a woman Ruth remembered being called Reheboth or something like that. Ruth still struggled with the Hebrew language and remembering so many new names.

A woman with a large growth on her nose slurped the vinegar and oil drink. The other women didn't seem to like her. "Well, that's all past now. This year promises to be a good crop. The barley is hanging heavy. Praise Jehovah."

The women nodded and grunted, grudgingly giving assent to the woman's observations. Apparently it was hard for them to agree with the one they disliked.

"Not that it will help Ruth and me. Don't know what I was thinking when I insisted that we walk all this way back," Naomi said with a sniff. "Not that I'm not thrilled to see you all again," she hastily added. "But how are the two of us going to live? No relatives to take care of us, no men to provide for us, abandoned by God. Just look at us; we're in a pathetic situation."

As the older women *tsked, tsked* sympathetically, Ruth quietly shook her head. She thought being in a familiar place, with old neighbors and homey customs, would hearten Naomi and rouse her plucky spirit. But Bethlehem just seemed to dispirit Naomi even more and give her the chance to voice her many complaints — especially her disappointment in God.

Now here Ruth sat, with a downhearted mother-in-law, little prospect for provision, and old, widowed neighbors who dropped by to sip and sigh. No, this wasn't how she had pictured Naomi's God would take care of them.

Setting the Stage

COMPLAINT DEPARTMENT

When life serves us delays and disappointments, like Naomi we can feel the need to unburden ourselves. But "talking it out" can easily turn into perpetual complaining — a habit that's hard to break, and an attitude that blocks our view of God's goodness and provision.

This week listen closely to people for one day. Observe what they complain about and the words they use to express their discontent. Write down the phrases that especially strike you as memorable. Keep track of your own complaints as well. Then evaluate the following:

- What seem to be the most common complaints?

- What do these comments tell you about what is important to us?

- Do people tend to complain about events they can control? Why or why not?

- What do the complaints expose about our view of God?

- What do the observations teach you about yourself and your complaining?

- As a result of concentrating on your complaints, what one thing would you change about yourself?

- How might this change affect your relationship with God?

Commit that one change to God and create a plan to institute some mouth and heart adjustments.

Discussing Ruth's Story

KEEP ON KEEPING ON

In this session we meet a despondent Naomi. Her challenge is to keep on going when heartache has pummeled her life and spirit. Ruth's challenge is to manage her own grief and culture shock while emotionally supporting Naomi. Both women need the faith to believe that God will provide for them, despite their feelings of despair.

Before you begin the discussion, read the Bible text, Ruth 1:19–22.

1. In this passage what would cause the townswomen to feel unsure whether the woman who stood before them was Naomi?

2. In verse 20, Naomi, whose name means "pleasant," insists that she be called Mara, which means "bitter." How would "Mara" respond to the idea that God would provide for her? To the thought of persevering in faith?

3. Read the Behind the Scenes section, "The Mighty Mountain," on page 33. If God is "Almighty" in Naomi's mind, how has she applied that word in a negative way toward God?

4. In what ways is she limiting God in verse 21? In what ways might she be giving God more "credit" than he deserves for the events of her life?

5. The Hebrew word translated "afflicted" can also mean "testified against." How does Naomi's negative view of God's role in the events of her life contradict what the Bible teaches about God's character?

6. How do you think Ruth feels as she stands by and listens to Naomi explain her plight to her old neighbors? What, if anything, would motivate her to persevere in this situation?

Behind the Scenes

THE MIGHTY MOUNTAIN

The Hebrew word for "Almighty" is *Shaddai*. Wrapped up in that word are the characteristics of strength, nourishment, satisfier of needs, and all-sufficiency. Some scholars believe the name is rooted in a word that means "mountain" and refers to "the One of the mountains."

The word is used forty-eight times in the Old Testament and eight in the New Testament. God employs it to describe himself to Abraham when the Almighty covenants (or makes a contract) with Abraham to make him a father of many nations (Genesis 17:1). When Isaac blessed Jacob, Isaac said, "May God Almighty bless you and make you fruitful and increase your numbers until you become a community of peoples" (Genesis 28:3). In this way, Isaac calls on a powerful and nourishing God to accomplish the blessing.

Job uses the name "the Almighty" in much the same way as Naomi does. In Job 27:2, he speaks of "the Almighty, who has made me taste bitterness of soul." Yet Job affirms his faith in the rest of the chapter. "As long as I have life within me, the breath of God in my nostrils, my lips will not speak wickedness [toward God]" (verses 3–4).

Shaddai is used to refer to the powerful God who brings judgment. In Joel 1:15, the prophet says the Almighty will bring destruction to Israel, and in Revelation 16:14 "God Almighty" will fight the demon spirits and kings of the world in the final battle.

BELIEVING THE BEST

We all, like Ruth and Naomi, face the severe challenge of believing the best of God when harsh weather sets in and doesn't move on. Doubts buffet us and questions assail us: Can we trust God? Will he provide? How will he care for us? When will he rescue us — and how does he define "rescue"? The cold winds of adversity whip about our faith and cause us to feel vulnerable and exposed.

How do we believe the best of God — and keep persevering — during such times?

1. Brainstorm sayings people use when times get tough such as "Every cloud has a silver lining," or "It's darkest just before the dawn." What do you appreciate behind the sentiment in these sayings? What about them bothers you?

2. List the choices we can make during ongoing adversity, such as praying, whining, believing good of God. Put a check mark by those that honor God, a minus sign by those that don't, and a question mark by those you aren't sure about. What keeps us from making the "check mark" choices?

3. Which of God's characteristics are hardest for you to believe in when difficult times seem unending? Why is it hard to believe in this quality?

4. While waiting for God's provision, what would tempt you to give up on him and the difficult situation you're in?

5. What would encourage you to persevere while waiting for God to rescue you? If time allows, recall biblical characters (e.g., Joshua at Jericho, David fighting Goliath, etc.) or others who persevered and received the provision they needed. What from their stories could encourage you to "keep on keeping on"?

6. When adversity seems unending, how can you keep a good perspective on God and his promise to provide?

When the storms of life toss about our boat, we cast around for a stabilizer of any sort. Often we forget he's already in the boat with us, wanting to calm us and rebuke the terrorizing winds of circumstances.

HUG ONE ANOTHER

Sometimes one of the most effective ways we can comfort one another is, in silence, to hug each other. Pair off for prayer. Express one thing that weighs heavy on your heart. Then take turns holding hands or hugging each other. Silently pray for that person as you hold her. Then pray a short prayer aloud for your partner.

PREPARING FOR BAD WEATHER

With a friend: When hardship enters our lives, it helps to be prepared and to find some reason to laugh — no matter how small that reason might seem. If the weather is "frightful" today, do something "delightful" with a friend to help take the edge off the weather.

You might don boots and stomp through the rain puddles or go outside and make snow angels. If the weather is delightful, prepare for a rainy (or snowy) day. Go shopping for bright colored umbrellas or mittens that delight your heart.

Afterwards, sit down for tea (iced or hot) and talk about how you can prepare for emotionally harsh weather and find laughter amidst the pain.

On your own: Study a biblical character's response to hardship and make note of how that person viewed God. You might look at Joseph (Genesis 45:4–8; 50:15–20), Paul (Acts 16:16–34), or Jesus (Hebrews 12:1–2) — or all three, if you have time. Also, check out how the person responded when circumstances went from bad to worse. For Joseph that would be Genesis 39; for Paul, 2 Corinthians 11:24–12:10; Jesus, Matthew 26:36–44. What seems to keep each of them believing good of God?

Then draw a picture in your prayer journal that depicts a hardship in your life. Write a prayer about that hardship. Remember that God will remain true to his character through it all, providing what you need to see you through the crisis.

Words to Remember

AFTER THE STORM

And the God of all grace, who called you to his eternal glory in Christ, after you have suffered a little while, will himself restore you and make you strong, firm and steadfast.

— 1 Peter 5:10

A Prepared Path

Combining faith with action equals provision.

*R*uth rubbed her sweaty hands on her skirt. *Something has to be done,* she thought. *And if anyone is going to do it, it has to be me.*

Naomi sat staring out the window, as she did every day. Was she remembering better days in Bethlehem, days when she was a wife and mother? Was she recalling the sorrow and loss of her husband and sons? Or was she recounting and lining up in a neat row, like planting a crop, the ways God had let her down?

One thing I know for sure: She's not thinking happy thoughts. Ruth frowned as she studied Naomi's profile.

A bird chirped merrily outside the window, and Ruth thought of how not too long ago she felt like that bird, happily singing as she prepared meals, washed clothes, and felt loved in the midst of Mahlon's family. The pleasant bustle of three women about the house had now changed to the lonely rustle of Ruth's skirts while Naomi just sat.

Naomi stirred from her memories and turned to Ruth as if at her daughter-in-law's bidding. Ruth urged words to form on her lips.

"Naomi, I have a plan." She looked into Naomi's eyes, which seemed clouded with sadness and bitterness.

"A plan? A plan for what?" Disinterest colored Naomi's questions.

"I've heard others talking about a Jewish custom." Ruth forced herself not to wrap her hands in the folds of her skirt. It was a nervous habit to keep her fingers occupied when she was fearful or uncertain. And she felt both.

"There are many Jewish customs, Ruth," Naomi's tired voice responded.

"Yes, but this one could put food on our table and help us to survive."

Naomi said nothing, as if survival were a bitter-tasting morsel to swallow.

Ruth continued. "Women go out into the fields and pick up whatever grain the harvesters drop. God's law makes provision for it. We could — "

"No! Ruth, it's dangerous!" Naomi's words snapped like a cloth being shaken free of crumbs. "You just don't know. Not every owner lets the women glean. Sometimes the women are beaten. Sometimes . . . worse things could happen to you, Ruth. I won't let you."

"But, Naomi, I must. We've used up all of our savings. We have only a little food left. I must do this."

Naomi turned back to stare out the window. Her shoulders slumped even lower than before. She pulled her shawl about them, as if to protect herself from Ruth's plan.

"Naomi, I must." Ruth's voice had fallen to a whisper.

Naomi's lips quivered. "Go then, my daughter, with my blessing."

Ruth nodded, put her hand on the doorknob, and prayed for Naomi's God to protect her. Taking a deep breath, she walked out the door.

Setting the Stage

TO ACT OR NOT TO ACT?

God sometimes uses unusual means to provide for his people. At times we only have to wait for God to act. But often, like Ruth, we need to take action to receive his provision, to find the path he has prepared for us.

Before this week's meeting, study the following passages and note what actions each individual took to receive God's provision.

Judges 7:1–23 (Gideon)
2 Kings 4:1–7 (a prophet's widow)
Matthew 8:5–13 (a centurion)
Matthew 9:1–7 (a paralytic man)

From what you learned in these passages, consider the following questions.

- What do these incidents tell you about how faith and action work together?

- Why do you think God asks us to take action when we need provision?

- Why do you think God sometimes asks us to do nothing but wait?

Write down a provision you need from God. Ask him if you should take action or just wait. Then sit in silence for at least five minutes. Write down any impression or any sense of direction that occurs to you. Commit the results to God and this week take a small step of faith, either by acting or waiting.

THE TALK OF THE TOWN

Ruth finds herself in a precarious place. She's a widow without financial support; she has a grieving mother-in-law to care for; she lives in a foreign land with strange customs and a different religion. She could easily be paralyzed by fear, hiding in the house with Naomi, but she takes the initiative to provide for their future.

As Ruth takes action, her reputation precedes her . . . and so does God.

Before you begin the discussion, read the Bible text, Ruth 2:1–16.

1. Read the Scripture passage and the Behind the Scenes section, "On Society's Fringe," on page 42. Why did Ruth's circumstances make it especially necessary for God to provide for her?

2. How does Ruth contribute toward acquiring that provision? What obstacles might she need to overcome to take action?

3. In verses 6–9, why might Boaz particularly notice Ruth and make special provisions for her? Explore several reasons, including that she and Naomi seemed to be "the talk of the town."

4. What does Ruth's response to Boaz's generosity reveal about her (verses 10 and 13)? List several characteristics.

5. What does Boaz's blessing in verse 12 show about his understanding of God?

6. At this point, do you think Ruth understands that she has, as Boaz mentions in verse 12, taken refuge under God's wings? Why or why not?

Behind the Scenes

ON SOCIETY'S FRINGE

Mosaic law provided for those on the fringes of society by allowing them to glean the leftover grain in the fields after the harvesters completed their work. In Leviticus 19:9–10 and Deuteronomy 24:19, God orders landowners to express a spirit of generosity toward aliens, orphans, and widows by leaving some grain behind for them.

These three categories of people are often grouped together in Scripture, for they were frequently alienated from Jewish society and susceptible to oppression, injustice, and exploitation. Therefore, God is depicted as their male protector, and every Israelite was commanded by him to treat them justly. But that was not always the case. Those who gleaned the fields were especially vulnerable. Not every owner left a portion for the gleaners, and sometimes the women were raped or beaten by men working the fields.

Also worth noting is that the term *widow* holds a more specific meaning in Hebrew than in English. A widow was a woman whose husband and father-in-law were deceased and who had no son capable of providing for her. She functioned outside the social structure in which every female lived under the authority of some male; she was responsible to and for herself.

In Middle Assyrian Law, the state issued a document verifying the widow's new status, allowing the woman to act on her own behalf. Numbers 30:1–16 explains that the validity of a woman's vow ordinarily depended on the approval of either her father or husband. But a widow's vow stood on its own.

GOD'S SHELTERING WINGS

Ruth slipped under the refuge of God's wings as she went out, in faith, to glean the fields. Her story encourages us to faithfully believe our needs will be met as well — and to take action when it's appropriate.

1. What kinds of needs did God meet for Ruth? As a group, write them out on a pad of paper, including specific physical, emotional, spiritual, and other needs.

2. Which of Ruth's needs are similar to yours? Choose one and describe it to the group.

3. From Ruth's story so far, and from your response to question one as a group, write a summary statement about how God provides for our needs.

4. Like Ruth, what obstacles do you need to overcome to obtain God's provision? Make a group list. Then work back through the obstacle list, discussing how each one can be overcome. If time allows, cite a Bible verse that speaks to each obstacle.

5. How can we discern whether we are to take action to obtain our provision or whether we are to wait for it? Explain your answer. If time permits, you could share your Setting the Stage section on page 39.

6. Boaz tells Ruth that she has taken refuge under God's wings. As you take action to receive God's provision — or wait patiently for it — what does the image of being under God's wings mean to you?

Ruth seems to be taking tentative steps of faith, as if testing to see if God will care for her. How encouraging it is to us that he tucks her under protective wings, where all are safe and warm. It's just the place we're looking for!

Prayer Matters

LIFTING UP YOUR REQUESTS

If you feel comfortable, share with the group an area in which you need God's provision. Then pray Psalm 36:5–9 by reading it aloud together.

Afterwards, offer two-sentence prayers for specific requests. Try to tie the requests back to the verses of the psalm. For example, "As you've reminded us, Lord, your faithfulness is as high as the sky. I pray that Jean would experience that faithfulness as she waits for her prodigal son to return home."

After Hours

LIKE A MOTHER BIRD – AND A MOUNTAIN

With a friend: God as a mama bird is a very comforting image. (See Psalm 61:4.) Throughout nature mothers of all kinds remind us of how wonderfully care is provided for the young, naive, and vulnerable. Watch a nature program with a friend, taking special note of caring mothers. Afterwards, talk about the way you can relate the information to God's care for us.

On your own: Psalm 36:5–9 is rich with images of God. Write down God's characteristics in these verses and the imagery associated with each characteristic. (You might want to look at a variety of translations.) What additional kinds of imagery could be used for each characteristic? For example, God's righteousness could be solid, immovable, and unchangeable like a mountain. Write out your ideas.

How do each of these characteristics of God relate to his provision for you? Describe these relationships, then write a poem or prayer that reflects how you feel about God and his ability to provide for you. Or think of a hymn or song that reminds you of God's character and provision ("How Great Thou Art," for example) and sing it to him.

UNDER HIS WINGS

How priceless is your unfailing love!

Both high and low among men

find refuge in the shadow of your wings.

— Psalm 36:7

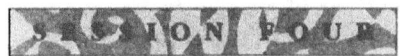

Unexpected Gifts

The Lord provides for us
in surprising ways.

*R*uth hummed as she walked toward town, away from the field where she had gleaned all day. The setting sun cast a rosy aura on everything and everyone. The bag of barley grain bumped against her leg and she smiled.

So much sun, so much grain, so much to smile about. She felt hopeful and realized it had been a long time since anything but emptiness had collected in her heart.

Thank you, God, she thought, and then felt surprised that her happiness expressed itself in a prayer. She wasn't used to praying. *But it* was *God who provided,* she insisted to herself. Boaz had said so.

The corners of her lips curved up farther as she remembered Boaz's kind eyes. They had sparked as he laughed during lunch. He seemed to find many reasons to be merry. She recalled how the field-workers had surreptitiously studied her while Boaz made sure her cup was always full of drink and that she had an ample pile of roasted wheat nuts. She had slipped a helping of those nuts in her pocket to present with a flourish to Naomi.

As she walked, she felt the bulge in her pocket to make sure the gift was still there. Then she caught sight of their house. *Please, God, let this perk up Naomi. You've provided so much for us today.*

But would a bagful of grain, a pocketful of nuts, and a promise of food for the winter be enough to lift Naomi from her doldrums? To enable her to see that God — the God Ruth had taken as her own — didn't hand out only hardship and heartache? As Ruth asked herself these questions she picked up the pace, ignoring how her back and arm muscles ached. She wanted to quickly reach home to tell Naomi all the ways Boaz had been generous to them today.

Then she spied Naomi at the window, just as she had left her that morning. Ruth lifted her hand in greeting, hoping Naomi would see it and somehow sense that God's hand had reached down to bless them. *Please, God, help Naomi to lift up her heart to you,* Ruth prayed.

Setting the Stage

SURPRISED BY JOY

Before this week's discussion time, recall two times you've been pleasantly surprised by someone. What made those surprises special? How did you feel about the people who surprised you? What do you think they were trying to communicate to you?

Now think about two times God has surprised you with something good. What made those surprises special? How did you feel about God as a result of them? What do you think God was trying to communicate to you?

Thank God for the element of surprise from both him and people.

Like Ruth, could you use a surprise from the Lord, especially in regard to provision for you? If so, pray and tell him about it. Specifically ask him for what you need, remembering the Lord's promise: "Ask and it will be given to you; seek and you will find; knock and the door will be opened to you. For everyone who asks receives; he who seeks finds; and to him who knocks, the door will be opened" (Matthew 7:7–8).

Write this promise on a card and decorate it as if it were a special gift. Then send the card to yourself and display it in a prominent place when it arrives. Each time you see the card, ask the Lord for the provision you need. Then wait for a door to open with God's surprise!

RUTH — *Trusting That God Will Provide for You*

A HOPE AND A FUTURE

As Ruth walked to the fields that first morning, she probably felt dread and fear. But God surprised her by touching Boaz's heart, and the wealthy landowner showed favor to the poor widow. Still, the Lord wasn't through with his surprises.

Before you begin the discussion, read the Bible text, Ruth 2:17–23.

1. Review the events of Ruth 2:17–23. What reasons did Naomi and Ruth have to celebrate? (Note: an ephah of grain is about twenty pounds.) Name more than the immediate provision God has given to them.

2. In verses 19 and 20 Naomi says two spontaneous blessings. What is similar about them? What is different? What do the blessings reveal about Naomi's heart?

3. Contrast Naomi's view of God in verse 20 with the view she expressed in Ruth 1:20–21. What do you think made the difference for Naomi?

4. Naomi refers to Boaz as one of their "kinsman-redeemers" and a "close relative" (verse 20). Read about the kinsman-redeemer in the Behind the Scenes section, "It's All Relative," on page 51. Later in Ruth 4:3 we learn that Naomi possessed land that once belonged to her husband. We don't know why she hadn't attempted to sell it yet. But based on Naomi's claim and the kinsman-redeemer role, what hope would a kinsman-redeemer — and the day's events — hold for the two women, in the present and also for the future?

5. What correlations can you draw between the ancient kinsman-redeemer and Christ's redemption of us? If needed, refer to Titus 2:13–14 and 1 Peter 1:18–19 about Christ's redemptive work. How could Boaz serve as a symbol of the Great Provider to come centuries later?

Sharing Your Story

PLEASANTLY UNPREDICTABLE

Our God is not capricious, but he's certainly not predictable. He seems to enjoy tossing surprise provisions our way as loving gifts to us. He's also interested in our response. When a surprise provision shows up, are we grateful confetti-tossers, like Naomi and Ruth, who rejoiced in God's provision, or inattentive party poopers?

Behind the Scenes

IT'S ALL RELATIVE

In ancient Israel God set up a system that provided for land to remain within a family (Leviticus 25:25, 47–49). The Israelites believed that Jehovah was the actual owner of the land he had given to his people for an inheritance, and they merely used it. That meant an "owner" couldn't sell the property just because he felt like it. He could offer it for sale only because of poverty. Even then, his nearest relative, called a "kinsman-redeemer," was duty bound to redeem or buy it back.

Should the nearest relative fail to fulfill his duty, the responsibility fell to the next closest kinsman-redeemer. Each kinsman-redeemer was asked to fulfill the role until one would do so. In this way a family financially "rescued" its members while keeping the property within its ownership. By law a relative's responsibility only applied to the land, but it was common for the kinsman-redeemer to marry his sister-in-law, if she had no children when she was widowed. Then the land passed to the woman's first son, born of the new marriage, but created "on behalf" of the dead husband.

If the land couldn't be bought back, it returned to the family in the next Year of Jubilee. Aside from providing financial freedom for those in debt, the Year of Jubilee was a "Sabbath rest" for the land, when it wasn't farmed, plus a time when the property returned to its original owners. It occurred every fifty years. This meant the land wasn't actually ever "sold." However, the land's yearly produce belonged to the temporary owner until the next Year of Jubilee.

1. Tell the group about one of the surprises from your Setting the Stage time on page 48. Describe what made it a pleasant surprise and how you responded to it.

2. How do you think God wants us to respond to his surprises?

3. What would be ways in which our response would disappoint him?

4. What do our responses to God's surprises reveal about us? About our relationship with him?

5. In what ways can you remember to "toss confetti" when God provides for you? Make a list, drawing from Naomi's response, observations, your experience, and creative ideas. It could be something as simple as singing a song of praise or as elaborate as throwing a party.

6. What role do you think our faith plays in God's surprising provisions?

Cultivating a receptive heart can make the difference between joyfully receiving God's bounty or mumbling about one's plight. So remember to toss confetti whenever God sends a surprise package with provisions in it.

Prayer Matters

YOU'RE INVITED

We receive invitations to all kinds of parties — baby showers, weddings, housewarmings, New Year's Eve celebrations. As a group write an invitation to God to surprise you with his provision and blessings. Then read that invitation aloud together as you begin your prayer time.

As you take turns praying, express some of your hopes for the ways God might bless and provide for you. Also mention some of your misgivings. Close with praises for his previous provisions and thanksgiving for his future grace.

IT'S A PARTY!

With a friend or as a group: Create a party for someone you suspect is feeling unloved and not provided for. It doesn't have to be an elaborate or expensive event; just think of ways to surprise the person with God's love. If no one comes to mind, you might throw a party at a retirement home or a hospital ward. Dress up as clowns. Serve popcorn. Bring balloons. Read a poem, prayer, or Scripture about God's love and provision. Celebrate our God of Surprises.

On your own: In your prayer journal or a single sheet of paper, record the provisions God has made for you this past week. Look to the week ahead and ask for his provision for specific needs. Meditate on Psalm 72:12–14 as a promise of God's provision. Then write a song of thanksgiving, set to a familiar tune, and sing it to God. Or listen to a favorite song on a CD and personalize the words as a praise to God.

On the same day next week, look back on God's provision for you. Were there any pleasant surprises? Thank him for them.

Words to Remember

A REASON TO SING

It is good to praise the LORD

and make music to your name, O Most High,

to proclaim your love in the morning

and your faithfulness at night. . . .

For you make me glad by your deeds, O LORD;

I sing for joy at the works of your hands.

—Psalm 92:1–2, 4

Carefully Covered

Sometimes God provides for
our needs through others.

*R*uth pulled a shawl over her head and held it tightly under her chin. The night air was chilly. As she knelt, hidden in the field, the barley sheaves surrounding her looked like ghostly bundles ready to tiptoe off to a warmer place. But they remained unmoving even as the breeze wisped through their tendrils. She would have liked to tiptoe off herself.

Straining her eyes, she studied the bundle lying on the stamped-down dirt of the threshing floor. This bundle didn't move any more than the barley sheaves. Straining her ears, she heard the steady breathing of one deep asleep.

Lord, bless me now as I plunge into my future, she prayed. Then swallowing hard, Ruth carefully stood up and crept over to the sleeping figure. Her skirt caught on a sheaf, which rustled noisily. She paused.

The steady breathing continued. No moon offered its light tonight, but she could see that Boaz lay on his back, his face a soft white above his bedding.

Please be kind to me, as you have in the past, she silently begged the man. There was so much she didn't understand about Jewish customs. How could she explain to herself what she was about to do? Her mother-in-law had told her this was appropriate and that Boaz would understand. That Ruth would be safe. That Boaz would not take advantage of her.

I want to believe these things. Naomi would never ask me to do something that would bring me harm. Yet, if Ruth's actions displeased Boaz, she could never glean in his fields again. And what if he told other owners? How could she, a Moabitess, ever gain standing in the community if other men knew about her deed tonight?

What if Boaz *did* take advantage of her? Only the two of them were in the field; she had no way to protect herself. And Naomi's instructions had seemed so, well, suggestive. Naomi had even insisted Ruth bathe and perfume herself before coming.

I won't do it, Ruth declared to herself.

As she turned to slip away from the field, Boaz stirred. She held her breath. It wouldn't do for him to wake and find her standing over him. She would have to explain everything to him then anyway.

Just do it. It's your best hope for a good future for you and for Naomi. You can't glean fields for the rest of your life. Trust Naomi. Trust God. God, yes, God has proven faithful and caring. I can trust him to do right by me.

Ruth knelt and felt until she found the corner of Boaz's heavy cover. As she nuzzled at Boaz's feet, she closed her eyes and thought, *Well, God, here goes . . . everything.*

Setting the Stage

ASKING FOR FAVORS

All sorts of emotions are attached to asking for a favor. This week before discussing Ruth's request with the group, recall the biggest favor you ever asked of someone.

- What forces prodded you to make the request?

- Was it hard to ask? Why?

- How did you decide whom to ask?

- Were there fears attached to the asking? If so, what were they?

- What responses did you envision?

- Did the person's response pleasantly or unpleasantly surprise you? If so, why?

- How did you feel about the person after you made your request?

- Did you thank the person in some special way?

Now turn all these questions to a time you asked God for something really big. What insights do you gain about your relationship to God? Write them down.

If you never offered God a special thanks, do so now. (Even if he responded with a no, he was expressing love to you.) For example, you might buy flowers for the altar at an upcoming church service or purchase one rose and place it in a beautiful vase in your home where you will see it often. Thank God for his goodness each time you look at it.

CAN YOU LEND ME YOUR BLANKET?

Naomi and Ruth both knew God's provision would last through the winter, but the long-term issues of survival were not resolved for them. Consequently, Naomi devised a plan that would depend on God providing through someone else. It's a place where God often puts us too.
Before you begin the discussion, read the Bible text, Ruth 3.

1. In this passage, in what ways does Naomi seem different from the past?

2. What misgivings might Ruth feel as she hears Naomi's plan in verses 2–4? After reading the Behind the Scenes section, "A Garment of Protection," on page 60, suggest how Naomi might respond to Ruth's fears and reservations.

3. What might Ruth's response in verses 5–6 tell us about her? About the women's need for provision?

4. Read verses 7–9. Why do you think Naomi sent Ruth to make this request rather than Naomi asking Boaz directly?

5. What do Boaz's comments in verses 10–11 tell us about his character?

6. Do you think Ruth and Boaz acted out of (a) love, (b) custom, (c) necessity, or (d) all of these? Explain your opinion.

7. Divide into pairs and think of a title of a popular or religious song that might have reflected Ruth's mindset as she sat at home waiting to find out whom she would marry (such as, "The Impossible Dream"). Then think of a title that represents Boaz's thoughts as he headed for town (such as "Get Me to the Church on Time"), and one for Naomi as she waited with Ruth (such as "Praise God from Whom All Blessings Flow"). Share your titles with the group and, if necessary, explain why you chose them.

Behind the Scenes

A GARMENT OF PROTECTION

To us, Naomi seems to have directed Ruth to be forward and presumptuous. But Naomi was well within Hebrew customs in her instructions. The correctness and acceptability of Naomi's guidance are reflected in Boaz's response. He was not puzzled or offended by this approach. Instead, he spread his garment over Ruth, which indicated he would protect her within the marriage relationship, should that responsibility fall to him. His comment regarding her choice to approach him, an older man, and his compliment of her noble character also show that he did not consider her actions as sexually suggestive.

The image of spreading the garment figuratively suggests Ruth's coming under the protective wing of Boaz. But even literally, the action is heartwarming. The garment refers to the corner of a bed covering — or its "wing" — which a man spreads over his wife and himself. (Also see Ezekiel 16:8, in which the "corner of the garment" is used.) In this way, Ruth asks Boaz to marry her and be her redeemer, and he accepts the responsibility, should a closer kinsman-redeemer decline it.

Ruth's request was based on the custom of combining two Mosaic laws: the marriage of a widow to her brother-in-law to beget a son who takes the name of the deceased brother, and the purchase of a family's land by the kinsman-redeemer. Hebrews expected the kinsman-redeemer to both marry the widow and purchase the land, even though the law did not require both actions.

Commentators suggest Ruth slept next to Boaz because it was late and a moonless night. It would have been difficult for Ruth to travel home until closer to dawn. Boaz is careful to protect Ruth's reputation, not wanting others to discover she had spent the night. If the other kinsman-redeemer chose to accept his duty and marry Ruth, Boaz would hand over the widow with her reputation unsullied.

RUTH — *Trusting That God Will Provide for You*

LEANING ON THE EVERLASTING ARMS

Ruth and Naomi probably started their trek from Moab to Bethlehem with very limited sight about how God might provide for them. Yet his loving arms enfolded the women, and his caring ways opened their eyes to how much he could do with so little. When we, too, possess little hope or faith, God asks us just to lean on him — and watch.

1. God provided for Ruth through Boaz, Naomi, and society. How has he used similar means of provision for you?

2. Who has God used to provide for you that surprised you the most? Why was it surprising?

3. Do you harbor misgivings about other people providing your needs? If so, what are they? How might Ruth's story help calm your misgivings?

4. Why would God sometimes ask us to wait for his provision?

5. What song title would express how you feel right now about God's providing for you through others?

Often after we've followed God's lead to a field of provision, crawled under the blanket of another to ask for help, and requested the Lord's care through it all, only one more thing is required of us — to wait for God's provision. And he is faithful to provide.

Prayer Matters

SINGING FROM THE HEART

Choose a song from one of those suggested from question five in Sharing Your Story. Sing that song as a prayer. Then pray for individual requests and close by singing the song again.

If you can't find a song everyone knows the words to, you could use the following hymn, "What a Friend We Have in Jesus."

What a friend we have in Jesus, all our sins and griefs to bear;
what a privilege to carry everything to God in prayer.
Oh, what peace we often forfeit, oh, what needless pain we bear —
all because we do not carry everything to God in prayer.

Are we weak and heavy laden, cumbered with a load of care?
Christ, the Savior, is our refuge; take it to the Lord in prayer.
Do your friends despise, forsake you? Take it to the Lord in prayer;
in His arms He'll take and shield you; you will find a solace there.

RUTH — *Trusting That God Will Provide for You*

PUZZLING OVER MATTERS

With a friend: Spend time putting together a jigsaw puzzle. As you do, talk about how working on a puzzle correlates with watching and waiting for God to provide for you. For example, you must wait to see how the pieces will fit together. You might want to work on two small puzzles with subjects that remind you of God's caring; then each of you could keep a puzzle afterwards.

On your own: God uses others to provide for us, but he also wants to use us to provide for others. So how about being someone else's provision? Working in a soup kitchen? Giving a small amount of money to someone, even if you don't have much? Taking groceries from your cupboard and giving them to someone? Choose one way you can provide for somebody this week. Then do it.

Words to Remember

ENDURING LOVE

Let those who fear the LORD say:

"His love endures forever."

In my anguish I cried to the LORD,

and he answered by setting me free.

—Psalm 118:4–5

Blessed Abundance

God often provides more
than we expect from him.

*R*uth watched from her chair as the neighborhood women huddled around Naomi. A glow emanated from her that came not from her white hair or the sun pouring in from the window, but from deep within.

"A beautiful baby for certain," Reheboth pronounced.

"Except for the way his hair sticks straight up. Have you ever seen such a thing?" the woman with the wart asked.

Naomi giggled — actually giggled. "He is beautiful. And his hair is going to be just fine."

"What's his name again?" another woman asked as she fingered the long, thick hair that stood on end like a black sheaf of wheat.

"Obed," Ruth quietly inserted. This was her first outing with the baby, and the walk into town had tired her. She was glad to sit quietly while Naomi's friends ogled Obed.

Ruth looked about the house — Naomi's house now, no longer Ruth's — and stifled a yawn. The baby had kept her up most of the night.

How strange to think I used to live here, she thought. The road she had traveled into town today was the same one that took her first to the fields and now back to Naomi, not with a bundle of grain but with a far better expression of God's care.

So much had changed quickly after the night she lay down at Boaz's feet. She smiled at the thought of those changes. Boaz was a kind and thoughtful husband. And Obed was so much more wonderful than Ruth had ever imagined. Her heart felt it would burst with love for him.

Obed's fist poked out of his blanket, and he waved his bunched hand wildly in the air. A squeak of a cry came from his rosebud mouth.

Ruth started forward, eager to calm her baby. It wouldn't do to have him fuss on his neighborhood debut. But Naomi said, "I know what to do, Ruth. After all, I did raise two sons myself." Naomi chuckled as she tucked Obed's head under her chin and hummed a soothing tune.

Obed quieted down.

All the women of the neighborhood, Ruth, and Naomi sighed in contentment. God had blessed them abundantly, more than Ruth could ever have imagined.

Setting the Stage

OUT OF CONTROL

Often in life, after we've done everything we can about a situation and given it to God, all that's left is to wait and see how he will work. That's when life is truly out of our control.

This week, think about times — past and present — when life zoomed out of control, especially in regard to provisions you have needed. Make a list of those major out-of-control events. Then create two columns on your sheet of paper. Label the first column "Dissonance" (which in musical terms means the clashing of chords), and write down how you feel when life is out of control and you desperately want that control back. Include actions you generally take when you're struggling to regain control.

Then label the second column "Harmony" (which musically means the combination of simultaneous musical notes in a pleasing chord), and write down how you feel when you can quietly and in harmony with God wait for the matter to be resolved. Ask God to give you insight to your responses as you work.

Now look back at the situations you listed at the top of your sheet. Place a minus sign by those in which you experienced disharmony or dissonance; a plus sign by those in which you experienced harmony; and a zigzagged line by those where you went in and out of harmony and disharmony. Circle the situations in which God gave you more than you had hoped or could have wished.

Over the entire exercise write a prayer in which you commit your future to God, asking him to help you to experience harmony but to enable you to be kind to yourself when dissonance fills your heart. Thank him for his love and abundant provision.

FROM DARK TO DAWN

In our last session we left Ruth at her house, waiting to see who her kinsman-redeemer would be. She didn't know it at the time, but she had passed through her dark days and moved into the dawn of a bright new era. But first Boaz had some dickering to do.

Before you begin the discussion, read the Bible text, Ruth 4.

1. When Boaz sat at the town gate where business was conducted, why do you think he waited so long — even after the discussion of the property — to bring up Ruth? See verses 1–5.

2. Read the elders' prayer in verses 11–12. Why might they refer to Rachel and Leah, two sisters married to Jacob (Genesis 30:1–22) and Perez, the son of Judah and Tamar, his daughter-in-law (Genesis 38), in their blessing?

3. Read the wishes the women offered to Naomi in verses 14–15 and the Behind the Scenes section, "Baby Blessings," on page 68. What is the significance of the blessing given to Naomi? Their praise of Ruth?

4. What do the elders' prayers and the women's wishes tell you about the community's values? You may want to refer to Psalm 127:3; 128:3.

5. Why do you think the book ends with the genealogy in verses 18–22?

6. Read Matthew 1:1–16. Why does this genealogy differ from the one at the end of Ruth?

7. Divide into three groups. Have each group create a birth announcement, with one group pretending it is Ruth, one group pretending it is Boaz, and the third group pretending it is Naomi. Discuss what the different approaches tell you about each of these characters and what that person has experienced.

Behind the Scenes

BABY BLESSINGS

The kinsman-redeemer the women speak of in Ruth 4:14 is not Boaz, but the newborn son. This baby was not just the son of Ruth, but was also considered the son of Naomi (verse 17). As such, he took away the reproach of childlessness from Naomi and brought the prospect of comforting her in the days to come and tending to his grandmother in her old age. In all these ways he was Naomi's deliverer. Also, his name, which means "servant," refers to Obed as the servant of God and as the "serving one" for his grandmother.

The women chose to compare Ruth to seven sons. The number seven denotes a large number of sons. A mother of many sons possessed much support for her old age and held the prospect of permanent continuance of her family. Through Ruth, Naomi had a son to replace her lost sons and the prospect of becoming the tribe-mother of a large and flourishing family.

Sharing Your Story

BLESSED BEYOND EXPECTATION

Talk about a happy ending! Naomi has seen God's abundant blessing; Ruth the foreigner has become part of David's and Jesus' lineage; and Boaz has gained a kind and God-fearing wife. But each of them had passed through a time of testing and faith expansion to end up in this spot. Along the way God provided what was needed — of course.

Sounds like our lives, doesn't it?

1. As you did for yourself in Setting the Stage, as a group list on the right-hand side of a page the hardships Naomi and Ruth experienced. Draw a line down the page, creating a second column. In the second column, mark behind each hardship a plus if the woman trusted God, a minus if she didn't, a zigzagged line if she wavered, and a question mark if you aren't sure. What does the list tell you about each woman's passage of faith?

2. Now list the types of provision God made for the women. Put a plus mark if God used other people to provide, a circle if God used the women themselves, and a circle with a plus mark if it was a combination. Use a star if God chose no agency but directly intervened. What does the list tell you about how God tends to provide for us?

3. Place a check mark in front of the items on the list that God provided in greater abundance than Naomi indicated she expected. Place an asterisk in front of those for which God made greater provision than Ruth expected. What does this tell you about God's generosity toward us?

4. What is the most important lesson you learn from Naomi? Ruth? Boaz?

Ruth's story — and Naomi's and Boaz's — gives us hope that we, too, will experience God's provision in extravagant ways. We're right to place our hopes in him. It's the safest place to tuck them.

Prayer Matters

PRAISES AND BLESSINGS

Like the men who blessed Boaz, pair off and bless one another. Create your own blessing to match your desires for your prayer partner.
    Or read this blessing:

"Lord, bless _____ and give her increased grace to hear and receive your Word and give her a heart to love and fear you. Inspire her in her calling to do the work you have given her to do with singleness of heart, as your servant. Comfort her as she needs comfort, strengthen her heart where it may be weak, enable her to rise up should she fall, and above all, give her the grace to look to you for provision to live a godly life."

Then, like the women who praised God with Naomi, spend time as a group praising God in prayer for his provision.

HIS BANNER OF LOVE

With a friend or as a group: Design and create a banner that expresses the chief lesson you've learned from the book of Ruth. Use symbols (such as a sheaf of barley) and depictions of everyday objects (such as a shoe that symbolized a pledge to keep one's word) as well as colors (blue to represent God's being "true blue" in his faithfulness) to represent the lesson. Take turns hanging the banner in your homes. (Note: the banner doesn't have to be big if you would rather create a smaller one. And you don't have to sew the banner. You could use a glue gun instead.) A simpler alternative would be to use construction paper on poster board.

On your own: The Book of Ruth is full of wonderful images that help to convey the underlying messages. Read through Ruth's story in one sitting and write down the images. Here are two to get you started: the road in chapter one, which symbolizes the different directions each woman chose; the grain in chapter two, which symbolizes the grain of hope God gave Naomi and Ruth.

After you've collected the images, write a poem or prayer to God using those images. Express to him the variety of emotions you feel as you experience hardship, wait for him to act on your behalf, take risky steps by faith, watch as he brings others into your life to provide, and receive the surprises of provision he slips in along the way. Be sure to use stickers, stamps, and your own art with the poem.

GOOD AND GREAT

Great is the LORD and most worthy of praise;

his greatness no one can fathom.

One generation will commend your works to another;

they will tell of your mighty acts. . . .

They will celebrate your abundant goodness

and joyfully sing of your righteousness.

— Psalm 145:3–4, 7

Leader's Guide

These guidelines and suggested answers can help enhance your group's effectiveness. However, remember that many questions require opinions rather than "right" or "wrong" answers. Input is provided only for those questions that may need additional insight.

To guide the group effectively, it helps to complete each session privately before you meet together. Then as you lead the group you can better facilitate the discussion by clarifying the questions when needed, offering suggestions if the conversation lags, drawing out members who aren't contributing much, redirecting the focus from participants who tend to dominate, and asking women for explanation when they contribute simple "yes" or "no" answers. Also, during the prayer time be sensitive to women who need encouragement or ideas for praying as a group.

For all of the sessions use a whiteboard, chalkboard, or easel pad for making lists and comments the entire group can observe. Also provide markers for writing.

SESSION ONE: *Tough Choices*

Objective: To realize that, even when hardships come, the most important choice is to believe God will provide for you.

Discussing Ruth's Story: Many Choices

2. This issue is hotly debated among theologians. Most seem to believe Elimelech was not acting out of faith as he exposed his family to the pagan ways of the Moabites, who worshiped the god Chemosh and offered their children as human sacrifices to this god. But Elimelech may have seen moving to Moab as God's provision that enabled Elimelech to care for his family. He may have never thought they would have to remain in Moab for ten years, during which time his sons were certain to choose wives. Both of these daughters-in-law seem to have been good

women who responded honorably and culturally appropriately when Naomi decided to return to Israel. As young widows, these women were expected to remain with their mother-in-law — even if their father-in-law and husbands died — for their families had made agreements that the women were to become part of their husbands' family. Considering Israel's own spiritual waywardness during this time, it was hardly a godly nation, but it did have God-oriented traditions and culture. As a group you may not agree about Elimelech's decision, but we, too, often must make decisions that are a mixture of faith and fear.

3. The following questions might help the press corps focus its interview. For Naomi, you might ask the following: Why are you going back to Bethlehem? How do you think you'll feel as you walk into Bethlehem for the first time in ten years? What will be the nicest thing about being back? What will be the hardest adjustment you'll have to make? How will you and your daughters-in-law provide for yourselves? What will you miss most about Moab?

     For Ruth and Orpah, you might ask the following: What will you miss most about Moab? What do you think will be the biggest adjustment for you? What are you looking forward to most? What do you predict your future will be like? Do you think you'll ever come back to Moab? What did your parents say when you told them you're leaving?

6. Ruth seems to respond to the idea of returning to Moab as turning her back on God. Her insistence on continuing to Israel is an expression of her affection and attachment to Naomi as well as a yearning to know the Israelite God. After living with this Jewish family, she has learned enough about God to want to embrace him more fully (which speaks highly of the faith the family must have quietly lived before Ruth). Ruth is saying she has just started to know God and does not want to be separated from him. Naomi sees the future and God's provision for the young women lying in their parents' homes and in their culture. She sees herself as abandoned by God and unable — spiritually or physically — to provide for them and their futures. Painful as the separation is, Orpah returns to the familiar and known, where logic would dictate her greatest hopes lie for a new husband and a family.

Sharing Your Story: Eenie, Meenie . . .

5. If time allows, use a Bible concordance and find a verse that refers to each additional characteristic that you list.

SESSION TWO: *Challenges Galore*

Objective: To see that often God asks us to remain steadfast in believing him for provision, even when we must wait for him to act.

Discussing Ruth's Story: Keep on Keeping On

1. Naomi must have changed quite a bit physically during the ten years away from her old neighborhood. And her dampened spirit probably was reflected in her physical appearance. It's also possible that she was much poorer than when she had left, which would be apparent in how she dressed. Also, that she is without her husband and two sons would mark her as much changed. Plus she now had a young Moabite woman with her. Scripture also indicates that widows wore special clothing (Genesis 38:19; 2 Samuel 14:2). All of these changes would cause the women to wonder if it truly was Naomi who stood before them.

3. Naomi probably feels God might be a sustaining mountain for others, but to her he's more like a mighty mountain blocking the sun. She may have spoken the name "Almighty" with sarcasm.

5. To testify against someone is to suggest that person has done something wrong that must be exposed and righted. Perhaps Naomi has a sense of God punishing her for something she has done. She doesn't seem able to see his love or that he was with her in her afflictions and still is. Bible verses that express who God is include the following: Deuteronomy 33:27a; 2 Samuel 22:17–20; Psalm 9:9.

SESSION THREE: *A Prepared Path*

Objective: To explore how God uses our faith-based actions to provide for us.

Discussing Ruth's Story: The Talk of the Town

3. Ruth would have stood out to Boaz as someone he had never seen before — a new face in town, which probably wasn't that

common an occurrence. Also, Ruth is a hard worker, taking only one break, which must have been unusual for the foreman to make note of it. In addition, Boaz would have known they were related as soon as the foreman identified Ruth.

5. Boaz acknowledges that Ruth has placed herself under God's wing, believing she will find refuge and provision there. Boaz believes God, who is good, will provide and protect.

6. Ruth wants to believe that what Boaz says is true. The passage's wording suggests that she believes it probably is.

Sharing Your Story: God's Sheltering Wings

4. Some verses might be Matthew 9:22; Ephesians 2:8; James 1:5–8; or 1 John 4:18.

SESSION FOUR: *Unexpected Gifts*

Objective: To discover that God
provides in ways we can't always predict.

Discussing Ruth's Story: A Hope and a Future

1. Ruth and Naomi now have a good supply of food, an invitation to glean through the wheat harvest as well as the barley, a safe field in which to work, and a connection with their kinsman-redeemer — and thereby hope for a long-term solution to their poverty, a husband for Ruth, and progeny for Naomi.

5. We, the "poor relations," have sold ourselves into slavery to sin. Our kinsman-redeemer, Christ, is duty bound to redeem us — with his blood rather than with money — from slavery. But, like the land, we never really belong to sin; we are still part of the family even before we reclaim that right through Christ's redemptive act on our behalf.

SESSION FIVE: *Carefully Covered*

Objective: To explore how God uses others to provide for us.

Discussing Ruth's Story: Can You Lend Me Your Blanket?

1. For the first time Naomi moves from passivity into taking an active role in their well-being. She offers to solve their prob-

lem. She seems self-assured and confident of the outcome. In Hebrew, her words communicate undoubted certainty. Apparently God's provisions have awakened in Naomi a belief that enables her to take specific and confident action.

3. Ruth displays a large degree of trust in Naomi, for Ruth probably didn't really understand how the Jewish custom worked. This also would seem to be an expression of her faith in Boaz and his integrity and in God, who had cared for Ruth and Naomi in such surprising ways already. But Ruth's willingness to obey also shows how desperately the women needed a long-term solution to everything that was lacking in their lives.

4. Naomi may have been afraid that she would fail if she asked Boaz directly. A kinsman-redeemer was required by duty to buy the family's land, but he was not bound to marry the widow, and this was Naomi's larger intent. It would be much more difficult for Boaz to say no to Ruth's approach.

5. Boaz is quick to reassure Ruth that he welcomes her suggestion. He shows he is concerned for her feelings and will deal with her with integrity. He admires her virtue in not pursuing younger men (which suggests Boaz was considerably older than Ruth). The kindness he refers to is the love and caring she has shown to her mother-in-law. And this additional kindness is taking the appropriate action of asking her kinsman-redeemer to care for her and to provide a son for her family through marriage. Boaz's response shows sensitivity and respect for Ruth. Boaz wants to do the right thing. He knows another man has first priority in the role of kinsman-redeemer, and he must give him the opportunity to fulfill this role. Thus Boaz shows himself to be a man of integrity. But Boaz tells Ruth that he will marry her if the closer relative fails to, which shows an understanding of the tension and vulnerability she must have felt. Rather than send her home in the middle of the night, he tells her to stay, which is an act of protectiveness. But, toward morning, he urges her to go so that no one will see she has been with him, resulting in her reputation being sullied. As a token of his intent to care and provide for her, he sends her home with barley. In all these ways, Boaz shows himself a kinsman-redeemer well suited to carry such a title.

Objective: To realize that God often provides beyond
what we thought possible.

Discussing Ruth's Story: From Dark to Dawn

1. Consistent with the integrity Boaz has shown throughout the
story, he presents the easiest portion of the package first: the
opportunity to purchase the land on Naomi's behalf. Boaz seems
to be doing everything he can to give the kinsman-redeemer an
opportunity to redeem the situation for Naomi and Ruth. This
offer is, of course, one that will cost the kinsman-redeemer
money because he must let the land remain with the person who
buys it until the Year of Jubilee. So the kinsman-redeemer must
pay out money to the current owner, who will continue to work
the land and gain from the produce until the Year of Jubilee. But
ultimately the land would belong to the kinsman-redeemer. Boaz
could have easily mentioned at the very start of the conversation
that the land was owned by Naomi *and Ruth*, but he chose not to
mention Ruth until the kinsman-redeemer made a commitment
to redeem the land. Boaz seems to want to give the kinsman-
redeemer every opportunity to agree to fully redeem the situation, not only to purchase the land but also to marry Ruth.

   Another way to read this passage is to see Boaz as protective. He entices the kinsman-redeemer to buy the land, from
which the kinsman-redeemer would have thought he eventually would profit, and then reveals that it's more complicated
than it first seemed. Not only must the land be purchased, but
a marriage is also involved — with the progeny of that marriage receiving the land. Perhaps Boaz is, in this way, testing
the character of the kinsman-redeemer. Is this man willing to
redeem the land for a son born to Ruth? Or is he interested in
redeeming the land so that he might own it someday?

   Since the story does not reveal Boaz's motives, either sce-
nario could be true. But Boaz, a man of considerable wealth
and presumably business acumen, may very well have chosen
this presentation to test the motives of the kinsman-redeemer.

2. The elders prayed that Ruth would "build up" Boaz's house
with children. To "have standing" would refer to begetting and

training worthy sons and daughters. To "be famous" is a phrase used only in this peculiar way in this verse and seems to mean to "make for yourself a well-established name through your marriage with Ruth, by a host of worthy sons who will make your name well-known." Perez was Boaz's ancestor, and the men of the city also wish Boaz a large family of his own such as Perez had. Tamar was like Ruth in that she was a childless widow. The elders also prayed for an honorable, fruitful family such as Jacob had through Rachel and Leah.

5. These final verses unveil one of the reasons the book was written: to show that David's ancestry was traced to Ruth the Moabitess and Boaz, two honorable people who looked to God for his provision and help. In fact, the Jews respected Ruth so much that the book of Ruth was read each year at the Feast of Weeks.

6. The passage in Matthew expands past listing David to show that Boaz and Ruth were in Christ's lineage as well. As a result, Ruth's position is elevated considerably. This connection to Christ is another way in which the book of Ruth shows how God blesses those who look to him for provision in ways they could never imagine.

   Also note that the Matthew passage includes five women: Tamar, who is listed as the wife of Judah; Rahab, who is listed as the mother of Boaz (which might explain his compassion for a foreigner since his mother, too, was a foreigner from a people who did not turn to God); Ruth; Bathsheba, who, as an adulteress, is listed as the wife of another man, not David; and Mary, Christ's mother. These women show how God took the lowly and despised and used them for his glory.

WOMEN OF FAITH™

Women of Faith partners with various Christian organizations,
including Zondervan, Campus Crusade for Christ International,
Crossings Book Club, Integrity Music, International Bible Society,
Partnerships, Inc., and World Vision
to provide spiritual resources for women.

For more information about Women of Faith
or to register for one of our nationwide conferences,
call 1-800-49-FAITH.
www.women-of-faith.com

8/99

Printed in the USA
CPSIA information can be obtained
at www.ICGtesting.com
JSHW012037060724
65970JS00005B/9